LIFESTYLE ARCHITECTURE

Coast

LIFESTYLE ARCHITECTURE

Coast

Text and photography by Janelle McCulloch

images
Publishing

Published in Australia in 2011 by
The Images Publishing Group Pty Ltd
ABN 89 059 734 431
6 Bastow Place, Mulgrave, Victoria 3170, Australia
Tel: +61 3 9561 5544 Fax: +61 3 9561 4860
books@imagespublishing.com
www.imagespublishing.com

National Library of Australia Cataloguing-in-Publication entry:

Author:	McCulloch, Janelle.
Title:	Coast: Lifestyle architecture.
Edition:	1st ed.
ISBN:	9781864703313 (hbk.)
Notes:	Includes index.
Subjects:	Seaside resorts—United States.
	Seaside architecture—United States.
Dewey Number:	647.940973

Edited by Debbie Fry

Designed by The Graphic Image Studio Pty Ltd, Mulgrave, Australia
www.tgis.com.au

Pre-publishing services by United Graphic Pte Ltd, Singapore
Printed on 140 gsm GoldEast Matt Art paper by Everbest Printing Co. Ltd., in Hong Kong/China

IMAGES has included on its website a page for special notices in relation to this and our other
publications. Please visit www.imagespublishing.com.

Contents

Introduction

BETWEEN THE SEA AND THE IMAGINATION
Architecture Designed for Living on the Edge

There is something about the potent combination of sand, sea, understated coastal landscapes, and the constant, almost hypnotic, ebb and flow of life on the edge of continents that inspires architects and designers to create extraordinary beach houses. It may be that the collection of these compelling elements somehow stirs up a high level of creativity in architects and designers. It may simply be that all that rejuvenating salt water, those ocean views and invigorating sea breezes shift the creative cobwebs to one side and allow the imagination to work again. It could even be the persuasive, perhaps unconscious, promise of spending time in such a restorative environment.

Whatever it is that draws architects and designers to the coast, their house designs, after they've spent some time staring out to sea, are almost always inspirational. No one can quite work out quite why, but beach architecture is some of the most poetic in the world. It is architecture in sonnet form.

The real answer, perhaps, lies in the landscape. Those who are privileged enough to own a piece of land by the sea realize very quickly that it will only remain serene if they keep it pristine and unaffected. An escape is only an escape if it reflects the idea of one. For this reason beach houses, by and large, do not stand on ceremony or dominate the landscape. Rather, they try to blend into the environment or "touch the landscape lightly". They leave small footprints on the land. Some architects believe that the simplest architecture is the beach umbrella: minimum footprint; maximum effect. Others believe beach architecture should be even simpler: think of driftwood sitting in the sand.

For these and other reasons, most beach houses tend to celebrate honesty of form and purity of line rather than aiming for the "wow" factor. This philosophy goes back to the original beach-side fibro shacks and their fisherman's hut neighbors, all of which were functional first and decorative second. The best beach houses do much with the least amount of effort; they create a poetic response to the coastal environment.

The elements, environment, and lifestyle that surround beach houses reinforce this "function first" philosophy. Architectural tools such as cross-ventilation, accordion shutters for light and sea breezes, flexible spaces, and informal rooms are not only included in designs but integral to them. Indeed, many architects believe that beach houses are planned from the outside-in.

Beach houses are also famous for being
places where the outside and inside
dissolve into each other.

Beach houses need to both embrace, and brace against, the landscape first and foremost. They can look good after that.

But beach houses are also famous for being places where the outside and inside dissolve into each other. Spaces flow easily and seamlessly together so that living rooms become decks, kitchens drift outside to outdoor barbecues, bathrooms extend to outdoor showers, and wraparound verandas extend from bedrooms via romantic, colonial-style shutters – the most seductive way of persuading you to wander out of your bedroom onto the deck and down to the sea before breakfast has even been thought of. Open floor plans also promote conversation and a languid, easy style of living: think of the timeless appeal of a deck, inspiring cocktails or card games late into the night while the surf pounds the distant beach.

More than any other building, beach houses encourage a revitalization of life. Even the traditional color palettes, such as white and pale blue, enhance their sense of serenity and inspire respite and reflection.

Coast celebrates the beauty of the humble beach house. Revealing some of the most extraordinary homes on America's East Coast, from historic sea captains' houses, weekend cottages and grand architectural treasures to contemporary escapes, seaside hideaways, and glamorous getaways, it is a selection of America's finest beach houses built or designed over the past two decades by some of the country's most renowned names.

It also illustrates, through lavish photography, the beauty of the beach: the luminous light; the seasons from summer through winter; the seaside villages; the swimming coves and their weather-worn signs; the salt-covered cottages and their endearing fences; the hedgerow-, pine-, or palm-lined roads; and the charming accoutrements you find in any beach place, from yachts to rowboats, surfboards, bikes, and boat shoes. And of course there are the classic colors, from fishing shack blue to lobster red, and timeless white, which show up on everything from the doors to the shutters, the yacht sails, the deck chairs, and the interior design.

A feast for beach lovers, architects, interior designers and anyone who just loves escaping to the coast, it is a tribute to seaside shelters, grand and small.

So come with us, as we remove our shoes and spend some time on the sand.

Janelle McCulloch

Tiny Hideaways

The Chic Beach Shack

TYBEE ISLAND

The very nature of a beach hideaway means it needs to be simple, with an architectural modesty and humility. It needs to have an easy, undemanding, uncomplicated feel. The very nature of a beach house means that it needs to be effortless to inhabit.

This tiny cottage, named Splash Shack, is the epitome of this simplicity. It is, quite simply, the vision of the perfect beach shack, even if it is slightly more luxurious than the term "shack" implies, and much more chic. As bright and as cheery as the morning sun over an empty beach, it is immediately inviting, thanks to airy rooms that flow into each other, a cool white and tangerine-bright color palette, and a simplicity that whispers of a good time.

The cottage is entered off a front porch – itself the picture of beach-shack beauty – and then via two front living rooms that have been dressed in oh-so-comfortable armchairs, sofas and chaise lounges. One of the living rooms features a two-way fireplace, which also opens to the dining room on the other side: the other has doors that open out to the porch for ease of summer living. There is a sweet white cottage kitchen and two fabulous beachy bedrooms, plus a pool out back to dive in to if you don't want to wander down to the beach.

The cottage has had several owners over the past few years, and all have stamped their mark (and love) on it. The property originally consisted of two cottages on separate parcels of land, each built some time in the 1930s, but both were pieced together years later to create the unusual home that Splash Shack is today. Rooms have been opened up, walls torn away, spaces repainted, and of course interiors redecorated. The result is a place that is now quite perfect – not only in size and structure but also in mood and aesthetic.

But perhaps the most charming thing about the Splash Shack is the color. Decorated by Jane Coslick, who is famous for her skill with both cottages and paint, the Splash Shack may seem like it's mostly a cool canvas of white, but look closely and you'll notice an unexpected explosion of heart-warming shades. Tin buckets on the porch (left for guests to collect shells in) have been painted in periwinkle blue; a bed has been dressed in rose petals and pale sky shades, another in turquoise; while an old armoire has been painted in a delightful layer of raspberry pink, which perfectly matches the striped towels on the railway carriage hooks nearby. The dining room, meanwhile, features a banquette seat dressed in the softest sea-blue

and pale green cushions, while the kitchen sports bright turquoise door handles and a fabulously fun turquoise curtain cover-up. There are also charming paintings, ceramics and baskets dotted here and there to add to the congenial atmosphere.

The Splash Shack is the kind of place you walk into and immediately wish you owned: beautifully beachy, blissfully easy, completely unfussy and utterly fun. If only all beach shacks were just like Splash.

For rental enquiries about Splash Shack, look up www.tybeecottages.com

As bright and as cheery as the
morning sun over an empty beach,
it is immediately inviting.

The Chic Weekender

TYBEE ISLAND

There's no other word for it: Bead Cottage is sweet. So sweet, it's almost an architectural dessert. Stick a cherry on top and it would be complete.

Located on the just-as-sweet island of Tybee off the coast of Savannah, Bead is one of those wee beach houses that grabs your heart the moment you enter the pea-green gate. This is no fancy-schmanzy, show-it-to-all-your-friends kind of place, but a tiny, oh-so-private hideaway that you hope-to-goodness no one finds out about – because then they'd all start traipsing across the bridge wanting a bed to stay.

Dating from 1938, Bead was bought as a simple beach house by designer Jane Coslick, who loved its chic simplicity and timeless style. Rather than upgrade it, she decided to retain its humble, gentle structure and simply add a couple of layers of extra charm. Walls were whitewashed or bead-boarded, furniture was picked up at thrift shops and then recovered in pale slipcovers and rooms were tweaked with beach touches: books here; fish-covered cushions there; turquoise towels over there. The result is a place that's so simple, it's pure chic.

The area outdoors is just as marvelous. The enclosed porch is a design lover's delight, with a vibrant, lime-green chaise to match the citrus-colored door and periwinkle-blue walls. There is also a gorgeous blue pool, which just needs fuchsia-pink lilos floating on its surface to complete the pretty picture. Even the garden is enchanting, with green windows cut into the fence to offer passers-by a peek into this fairytale domain.

For rental enquiries about Bead Cottage, look up www.tybeecottages.com

Bead was bought as a simple beach house by its owners, who loved its chic simplicity and its timeless style.

Bead Cottage has been decorated in the fresh, uplifting, coastal colors of the island it is set on – sea blue, lime green, citrus yellow, beach-umbrella orange and ice-cream white – all of which combine to create a seaside sanctuary that is both cheeky and sweet.

The Distinguished Boathouse

NANTUCKET

The Constitution Boathouse is a seriously handsome piece of property. Distinguished, dignified, straightforward (and also quite straight-backed) in line and style, it is the architectural version of a ship's captain – only a very dashing one, like Russell Crowe in *Master and Commander*, perhaps.

Sitting high above Nantucket Harbor, where it almost "floats" majestically above the landscape, the boathouse commands a prominent position on Old North Wharf, a wharf that is almost as striking as the architecture on it. All the boathouses and fishing buildings on this wharf were originally designed for more commonplace uses, until the land along the wharf was sold for residential use and savvy buyers converted the various dwellings, sheds and fisherman cottages into weekenders, guesthouses, principle places of residence, or just "boathouses with bang", as one Nantucket local put it. This boathouse was one of those to receive an upgrade of the most spectacular kind. "Boathouse" no longer seems quite the right term for it – it's almost like a "penthouse" now.

The property was intended to be a kind of weekender or getaway for its owner, who also owns a house in Nantucket town, just a few steps away. He wanted a place he could retreat to in order to read, work, entertain friends, or simply host guests when the overflow of summer visitors to his main Nantucket residence became too much.

Wanting a striking waterfront hideaway, the owner commissioned the Boston interior designer Gary McBournie to redo the interior, knowing that he was not only a part-time resident of the island, but also experienced in preserving historic Nantucket architecture. Gary McBournie has bought and updated half a dozen Nantucket homes over the years, and has established a reputation for creating beautiful homes out of neglected buildings. He has also established a reputation for preserving the soul and integrity of a house's architecture while at the same time imparting his signature "polish" and refined, classical style. Gary McBournie loves nothing more than taking on a good design challenge ("breathing life into a home is what I love doing best," he says), so when he was asked to update the Constitution Boathouse, he accepted the job with relish.

The problem is, boathouses are slightly different to townhouses, having been created for a different purpose. They also have a different floor plan: interiors often consist of just one room, and there are geographical constraints to

The boathouse is really an extension of the boat. It's meant to look like another galley and stateroom.

contend with too, such as harbors, and of course the sea. Gary McBournie, however, was cognizant of this, and embraced the one-room challenge with open arms, or paintbrushes.

Taking as his inspiration the fine lines and compact, elegant beauty of the owner's Hinckley Picnic boat, which is often moored at the boathouse's jetty, the designer decided to use the same shipshape style inside. "The boathouse is really an extension of the boat. It's meant to look like another galley and stateroom," he explains. Retaining the open space, he carved various corners out of the diminutive, minimalist interior through the use of charming sitting areas and boat-inspired design features. The kitchen, for example, is made from teak countertops, while the lattice cupboards echo those used on boats that allow much-needed ventilation while hiding all manner of appliances inside. And then there is the sitting area, which has been made by redesigning two ship's bunks into delightful banquettes.

Other spaces include a loft area for sleeping that looks like a lovely berth; a beautifully decked-out study (if you'll forgive the pun) that's been carved out of a room behind the kitchen; a smartly attired downstairs bathroom; and a breezy, colorful living room that forms the main relaxation space at the front, facing the water.

It's an idyllic retreat, made even more so by the extensive deck that unfolds from the living room and kitchen to the wharf outside. Here, outdoor tables and chaise lounges offer a place for dining, reading or simply watching the ferries drop off tourists, day after sunny day.

But the boathouse is also idyllic because it hasn't been gussied up too much. It may have the features of a penthouse – the electronic gadgetry in the study and the brand new appliances in the kitchen among them – but it

doesn't have a sense of pretension. It's not Versailles, after all. Gary McBournie was adamant that it should retain the humility and simplicity of a boathouse, so he kept many of the original features including the rustic beams in the kitchen ceiling. He also left the floors unadorned and simply painted them in an appealing marine-inspired shade of deck paint, then spattered them with red, white and tan specks to "roughen" them up a little. The effect is instantly enchanting. It looks like a boathouse should, which also means that dirt, water, or muddy shoes don't matter at all when they're traipsed into the space.

It's a boathouse that doesn't take itself too seriously. While much of it looks like a ship's stateroom, it's still got the winking cheeriness and rustic charms of a boathouse. And that suits the owner – and his delighted guests – just fine.

The Glamorous Getaway

TYBEE ISLAND

It's always intriguing to see how interior designers decorate their own homes. It's fascinating to see what fixtures, fittings, finishes, and furnishing they use for their own personal spaces, and just how flamboyant or bold they are prepared to be.

Jane Coslick's house is not only a fitting reflection of her skills as a designer of enormous talent, but also a beautiful snapshot of a house that treads a perfect design line between the "wow" factor and a warm and welcoming home.

Located on the island that's known to locals as only "Tybee", a tiny stretch of sand, sea breezes and simple beach houses situated off the coast of Savannah, this house was one of the most neglected and forgotten-about properties ever seen. The unusual curves of the house – art deco meets Miami-on-speed – meant that nobody could see past the strange architecture and hideous lines. Then Jane Coslick came along.

Already known for her work as a designer who specialized in restoring and conserving old homes, she had cycled past the property many times and had noted its neglected front yard and tired old façade. But the place seemed uninhabitable, even to her visionary eyes.

Then she became aware of the low price the property's owner was asking, and the designer couldn't help herself. She closed her eyes and wrote her name on the dotted line.

"It was one of the cheapest houses on the island, but you could tell why!" she says, still shaking her head at the boldness of the buy.

To say it was a "challenge" would be to utilize a rather overused word in decorating and design. The house was a mess, and at times a bulldozer seemed the only way out of the mire. But Jane Coslick is not one to give up easily.

She refashioned the front façade where the curved wall had thrown other buyers off, and recreated the half-moon room as a wonderful sunroom, full of apple-green chaise lounges and whimsical ephemera (a faux green parrot, for example, sits atop a tall cage festooned with a black-and-white polka dot bow), befitting its unusual design. A connecting kitchen, dining and living room were crafted on the other side of the house, while a bedroom, study and bathroom were created out of the mess of the rest. In the rear, a guests bedroom and a tiny reading nook offer further places to escape. The main color palette is black and white, which gives the spaces a crisp sophistication, but it's

kept from being too buttoned-up and refined (it is a beach house, after all) by quirky Jane Coslick designs. For example, a monochrome print of a palm tree in a thick Gothic-style frame offers an eye-catching feature in the timber-panelled kitchen, while footstools and ottomans are upholstered in zebra-print fabrics, and then painted in vibrant turquoise shades. "It's like putting a party dress on a house's architecture," says the designer of her witty ways.

The most remarkable changes, however, occurred in the rear yard. A lover of gardens, and places to sit in them, Jane Coslick installed a Balinese-style daybed, draped with romantic layers; built a guest cottage that resembled an exquisite doll's house; and then created an outdoor entertaining area with "windows", complete with curtains, that open through an ivy-covered wall into the neighbor's domain. (Luckily, they were as enamored with her style as everyone else is.)

It is a house that has kept its authenticity while being updated for a modern age. It is also quirky while still being entirely liveable. In fact, the property's facelift has been so successful that others passing by on their bikes often stop and say: "Now why didn't I think of that?"

And as for Jane Coslick, the Curve House has wrapped its curves around her and her husband's hearts. After causing so many raised eyebrows, hair-pulling moments, and agonizing days, the once neglected and eccentric old house is now very much their family home.

It's a beautiful snapshot of a house that treads a perfect design line between the "wow" factor and a warm and welcoming home.

The Hollywood Couple's Cottage

MARTHA'S VINEYARD

The Mermaid Boathouse is not the sort of island hideaway you expect two high-powered Hollywood producers to own. For a start, while it's on Martha's Vineyard, arguably one of the world's most famous summer playgrounds, it's not located in the center of all the action, amid the black-and-white elegance of Edgartown's historic architecture or the flamboyant color of Oak Bluffs. Neither does it command an imposing spot on the waterfront, like many of the old whaling captains' mansions and modern architectural homes. Instead, it's hidden away on a private one-acre lot down a charming lane in an undisturbed corner of the island; a lane that looks more rural Sweden or the Cotswolds than coastal Cape Cod.

It's so picture-perfect in its serenity that it looks like a movie ideal of a sea captain's home carved out of plywood for a Hollywood film. (Steven Spielberg actually chose the area and one of the neighbor's houses as the home of Roy Scheider's character, Martin Brody, in the movie *Jaws*.)

The charm of the lane and the endearing simplicity of the property appealed strongly to its owners, who were looking for a restful beach retreat that was blissfully far from the maddening crowds of LA. Purchased in 2003 by producers and husband-and-wife team Jill and Scott, owners of Aerodrome Pictures in LA, it was designed to be a place where they could really escape the pressures of work and LA physically, mentally, and aesthetically. It was also a gentle link to America's East Coast, which is where Jill, a Boston native, hails from.

The architectural austerity of the property is not an accident: in a former life the house was a 1940s oceanfront boathouse for a neighbor's property, before it was transferred to this sublimely pretty sliver of land beside Crystal Lake and behind the East Chop beach in the 1970s.

Having already fallen in love with the natural beauty of the island through having rented properties here over time, Jill and Scott were keen to buy something of their own. When they discovered this property was for sale, they snapped it up. Eager to retain the original bones of the boathouse and keep the place true to its origins, they decided to do a light restoration rather than knock it down and build a new house in its place.

"Our vision for the place was to have a sweet summer cottage that would evolve over the years," says Jill, who has embellished it bit by bit.

Rather than embark on a complicated and expensive overhaul that could potentially destroy the integrity of the house, she decided to simply whitewash the exterior and repaint the knotty pine walls in white. With a firm vision of what the cottage should feel and look like ("we wanted something open and airy"), Jill hired Martha's Vineyard designer Molly Finklestein, co-owner of the store Nochi in Vineyard Haven, to finish decorating the interior. The brief was to preserve the simplicity, and to create a cool, calm, cheery refuge for all those who visited.

Jill and Molly decided to make the dominant color palette white, using at least six different shades of it throughout the cottage. This gave reference to the marine whites of the island – the yacht sails drifting past, the swans on the lake, and the morning light over the beach – but also allowed the serene seaside views to be the central focus, rather than what was inside. (Occasional bolts of color are provided by cushions and pillows, and by artwork that features local Vineyard artists such as Kara Taylor and Peter Plamondon.)

The floor plan is basic, and because the space is quite small, it was a challenge to create unique and private spots throughout the

Its open-plan simplicity is perfect for beach-house life.

property. Jill felt that it was important to create such "nooks", for reading and working as well as private moments, but she also knew it was important to create as many sleeping areas as possible, both for guests and for those who chose to rent the house while they were away in LA. So they took the empty loft area that had been used for storage, and built a new wall that separated the space from the area below. This enabled them to create an additional bedroom with two twin beds in the new mezzanine area. When Jill and Scott returned to LA, Molly went to work on renovating the rest of the boathouse, installing and whitewashing bead board cabinets and butcher block counters in the kitchen.

The rest of the house was left alone, as its open-plan simplicity is perfect for beach-house life. There is a main living / dining room that extends along the length of the house, a pretty little kitchen, and two cozy bedrooms tucked out the back, plus the mezzanine loft space up top. The windows of the main living area face both the pond and the sea, and a deck extends the viewing opportunities out even further. In summer, when the garden is lush and green and the skies stretch on in an appealing canvas of blue, the deck is utilized constantly. And in winter, when the fire is burning and the surf is pounding in the distance, the view across the frozen lake to a mist-shrouded beach is just as romantic.

The interior decorating follows the "simplicity" philosophy, which was Molly and Jill's plan – the aesthetic is less about "design" and more about creating a family home. As such, the rooms are full of detail, interest, and personality – which is really what a good beach house is all about. Many of the pieces are antiques or thrift-shop finds – antique dressers discovered at flea markets and so forth – that have been redressed in splendid fashion, while others are the owners' treasures – old binoculars, tins, and vintage Vineyard postcards and maps, all

carefully chosen to fit in with the beach house aesthetic. Molly also installed a fabulous flowered chandelier over the dining table.

But while parts of the house are movie-perfect, there are other corners that are unexpectedly sweet. There is an outdoor shower, for example, which is labeled with a gorgeous old retro sign; two white Adirondack chairs are positioned right in front of the ever-changing view of ducks and waving pussy willows; and of course the requisite hammock is present, slung under a wonderful old tree.

It is a perfect island hideaway: a place for repose, respite, and contemplation. In short, it's the ideal Vineyard getaway, far from sharks, cinematic drama, and summer madness.

Martin Brody would have loved it.

For enquiries about Mermaid Boathouse, please contact www.aerodrome.com/Mermaid_Boathouse.

The Milliner's Studio

NANTUCKET

Darcy Creech's house, tucked away down a tiny pedestrian lane in the middle of Nantucket's historic district, is heralded by an enormous black top hat in the street. It's a tall, handsome hat, which tells you that something quite special is located at the end of this lane. When you reach the house, you know the hat was right.

Darcy Creech is a milliner, designing under the name Peter Beaton, who made her name when she designed Hillary Clinton's inauguration hat. Since then, her hats have been seen on many celebrities, including Martha Stewart. Darcy's hats are so famous, they've almost become celebrities in themselves.

The house where Darcy Creech lives is rather like a top hat itself: tall, compact, with simple, striking lines. More of a townhouse than a beach house, it is nonetheless located – like many of the houses in this part of Nantucket – only a few blocks from the ocean, and a beach theme runs right throughout the interior. Tiny children's swimsuits in vintage styles, for example, are hung like an artwork on one wall.

The house wasn't quite as admirable when Darcy Creech bought it. In fact, it looked more like a weathered old fisherman's cottage than a functioning modern home. But the price was right – this was long before Nantucket's house prices went hightide – and so the designer took the plunge. She had long wanted to move to the island with her sons (the name of her business, Peter Beaton Hat Studio, is actually taken from the name of one of her sons), and this property represented a watershed in her life. So she hired the contractors, and set about creating her new surrounds.

Previously, the house had consisted of several dark and gloomy rooms, arranged in traditional Nantucket style with a fireplace fronting the main entrance hall / room. Darcy organized for the contractors to "switch" the fireplace around to the room behind it, repositioned the stairs to the second floor, and opened the place up with windows galore. Then she sanded the floors so they fitted in with a beach-house aesthetic, built floor-to-ceiling bookshelves, and installed a black-and-white country-style kitchen. The effect was immediate. The house seemed suddenly airier, more open, and far more sophisticated. It also allowed Darcy to have her showroom / store / studio in the former entrance hall / living room while maintaining the privacy of the rest of her home.

The house where Darcy Creech lives is rather like a top hat itself: tall, compact, with simple, striking lines.

When it came to decorating, she called upon her favorite colors, which are reminiscent of Nantucket and its nautical style; namely white, black, and navy blue. Two sofas, slipcovered in navy-and-white stripes, found a home beside the elegant black-and-white fireplace; white window seats were built to complement the handsome bookshelves and cabinets; and even the colorful rows of her sons' caps and coats appear chic against an all-white wall.

But perhaps the most exquisite thing about this house is the studio and showroom: a space festooned with hats, brims and ribbons, all of them seemingly matching in a clever and harmonious way.

The Darcy residence is very Nantucket, both in design and in style. Milliner Darcy Creech is known for being able to adeptly reinvent the classics. This house is testament to that.

The Photogenic Boathouse

NANTUCKET

If boathouses were celebrities, peered at, pointed at, and photographed for their exquisite beauty and eye-catching attributes, then this would be one of the A-listers – the Jennifer Aniston of boathouses. Located on Nantucket, an island off the coast of Cape Cod that is itself not short on glamour, grandeur, and seaside grace, Lydia Boathouse commands one of the best positions on the island, right on Old North Wharf in the center of the town. In fact, it's possibly one of the best positions for a beach house or boat shed anywhere on America's East Coast.

The harbor is so close that the water laps at the boathouse's supporting stumps. There is a tiny ladder that drops down into the sea for those who want an early morning swim, and there is an equally tiny pier that extends out to offer shelter for a boat for those who wish to arrive by watery means. There is also a private park to the side of the boathouse, which provides a verdant space to stretch the deck chairs out and survey the watercrafts coming and going. To the rear, a picturesque lane offers more architectural and seaside delights in the form of a sequence of charming boathouses, each more photogenic than the last.

It's a place where you can sit back, put your feet up, and watch the boats chugging past.

Nantucket's Old North Wharf is almost as old as the island itself, and has changed almost as much as the island over the years. With one transformation after the other, there was a chance the spirit of the old wharf would be lost, trampled under the footprints of developers and tourists. Thankfully, this has not happened. Great pains have been taken to preserve the beauty, integrity, and historic charm of the wharf and its myriad boathouses.

Lydia is one of the first of these on the wharf, and also one of the smallest. But it also boasts the best position, right beside the tiny harbor-front park that you walk through to reach the boathouse's front door.

The property is so tiny it consists of just three rooms: a single room that is both a living room and a bedroom, a kitchen, and a bathroom. The interior roofline, however, soars to a "V", extending the space upwards, while French doors open out to a waterfront deck to extend the sense of space further.

The materials are as humble as the day the boathouse was built: timber beams, tongue-and-groove walls, and a basic wooden floor. The furniture, meanwhile, has been chosen for functionality rather than beauty. Both materials and furniture work perfectly in this space, giving it a sense of comfort. It's a place where you can sit back, put your feet up, and watch the boats chugging past. It's a place of peace, tranquility, and utter calm.

Now if only those pesky photographers would stay a little bit further away…

For enquiries about Lydia Boathouse, contact www.nantucketonline.com or www.greatpointproperties.com

The Seaside Hideaway

TYBEE ISLAND

If one had to name the most important ingredients for an idyllic seaside hideaway, the list might include an enchanting cottage that is easygoing and low-maintenance, a rooftop deck for sunset and sunrise inspections, a congenial porch for delightful cocktail hours, an oversized hammock for afternoon siestas, and a position close to the beach so that a swim before breakfast is as easy as stumbling out of bed.

How difficult is it to achieve these elements? Not difficult at all, judging by this cheeky property – 99 Steps has them all.

Known as 99 Steps because it is exactly that far to the beach – walk 100 steps and you'd just about be in the sea – this postcard-pretty home is like an exquisite doll's house, blown up to adult size. Owned and restored by Tybee Island conservationist and interior designer Jane Coslick, who has rescued, relocated, or restored more than 30 cottages on this charming island, 99 Steps is an example of what you can do with a little love and a whole lot of paint. Originally temporary housing for the corps of army engineers who built the first road onto Tybee Island, the 1920s cottage was purchased in 1992 by the designer – she stumbled across it one day, noted its proximity to the beach, and fell in love with its whimsical – and slightly wonky – architectural flaws.

This postcarc-pretty home is like an exquisite doll's house, blown up to adult size.

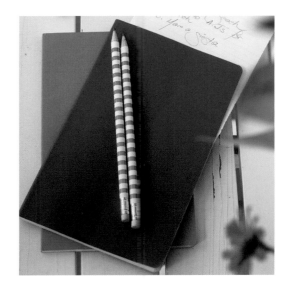

Envisaging a charming hideaway with a porch to sit on and a view of the sea, she immediately set about restoring the badly neglected, weatherworn old home – which, until then, had been considered by many to be a "tear-down".

First came the rejuvenation of the interior and ceiling, which were lined in white planks of timber and exposed rafters, and then came the pocket windows, which were repainted in an eye-catching shade of periwinkle blue (one of Jane's signature paint shades).

Jane then painted the pine floors, covering the porch in more layers of a Caribbean-inspired hue, and fixed up the Widow's Walk (an architectural term for a railed rooftop platform or lookout). She also enclosed the porch, which faces the dunes, and dressed it in bright yellow-and-white-striped drapes, comfortable cane and wooden chairs, and a huge white rope hammock so that it became a sheltered exterior "room", ideal for sitting back and listening to the ocean roar. ("You can't beat a porch. You just can't," she explains. "I had a client once who didn't want to build a porch. I said, 'Well, don't come to Tybee.'")

Determined to retain the "cottage" feel of the place, she tried to keep as many of the quaint architectural features as she could, and simply

added a layer of loveliness in the form of the periwinkle-blue floors and fuchsia-pink doors. She then filled the house with endearing vintage pieces and a truck-load of whimsical and irresistible accessories, including striped rugs in fairground colors; Adirondack deckchairs in turquoise, lime and yellow; bed linens in bright pinks and sunny yellows; and cute old weathered beach signs in myriad paint box shades.

Jane Coslick is famous for her preservation skills, and 99 Steps is a prime example. It is such an engaging little place, full of character and personality, and now so close to Jane's heart, that she has been reluctant to sell it all these years, even while other projects and properties have come and gone.

It has also become an icon of Tybee Island. 99 Steps may only be a humble cottage a heartbeat from the beach, but it is now firmly part of the landscape and soul of this much-loved island paradise.

For rental enquiries about 99 Steps, look up www.tybeecottages.com

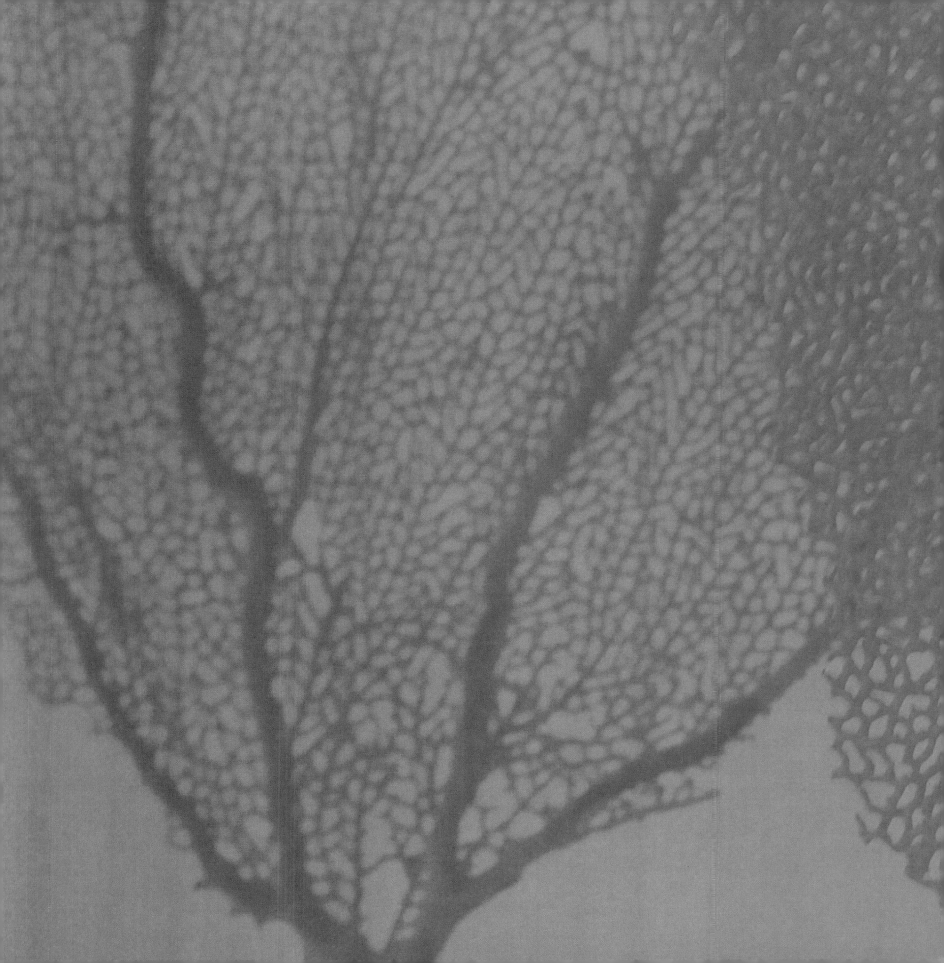

Island Refuges

The Black and White Beach Retreat

SHELTER ISLAND, LONG ISLAND

Architects can often neglect their own homes. It's a professional hazard, like dentists forgetting to check their own teeth, or mechanics disregarding their cars. Steve Schappacher, however, is different. His house shines with his attention to detail – although this could also be his wife's influence.

Schappacher and his stylist / designer wife, Rhea White, are the duo behind SchappacherWhite, a design studio based in New York with an office on Shelter Island. A small firm, they are fast establishing a reputation for grand glamour.

Several years ago, they were seeking an escape on Long Island, which is where many New Yorker go when they want a break from Manhattan's pace and madness. Bypassing the usual suspects – East Hampton, Montauk, even Sag Harbor – they found themselves aboard a ferry to Shelter Island. It was here that they experienced a kind of architectural epiphany.

Shelter Island isn't like the rest of the Hamptons or Long Island. It's not flashy. It doesn't encourage fast cars. And the only place you're likely to see brazen bikinis is at Sunset Beach, Andre Balzac's whimsical but mostly understated hotel on the north side of the island. Shelter Island is for those who want,

well, shelter – those who want peace and quiet, not loud, look-at-me style.

When the design duo stumbled across this 1904 cottage, they took one look at its serene location, its expanse of land out the back, and its potential to be so much more, and decided to buy. While they return to New York occasionally, they've never looked back.

Undertaking the renovations of the cottage was a major project, but the two – who share a similar design aesthetic – never wavered in their belief. They embarked on a renovation that virtually gutted the interior and made it brighter, more stylish, and far more spacious. New floors and walls were installed new bathrooms were crafted, a kitchen was created, and structural foundation work was strengthened. They then opened it up to the exterior by linking it with external porches and an elongated pergola that runs to a freestanding fireplace. Lastly, they added a swimming pool and turned the existing barn into a pool house. The change was amazing.

Half of the change was architectural, and the credit for that goes to Steve Schappacher. But the other half focused on interior design, and the credit for that must go to his wife. Rhea White is a marvel at making spaces look

extraordinary, and for this, her own home, she did more than merely whitewash floors, slipcover furniture, and put in jute rugs and awning stripes. She created a whole new style of interior design: think black and white beach glamour layered over Shelter Island simplicity.

"The house is small, and so care had to be taken with the scale of the furniture, so it didn't overwhelm the rooms and make them feel crowded," she explains. "However, we also wanted to bring a sense of boldness into the design, and tried to achieve this with the graphic quality of the stripes and the black / white color combo."

Being pragmatic souls, they also knew their beach house would be invaded by friends and family, and that it would be subject to "lots of sandy feet and swimsuits". So they tried to make the house as practical as possible with

pared-back floorboards, entrances with ample coat hooks, and various easily accessed "chill-out" spaces. The pergola, reached via either the gate or the living room, is one; the pool house is another, and the hammock slung between two tall trees is a third.

As it all came together, the house became a culmination of their talents, but it also became a summary of the things they loved – including personal, beach-themed mementos like feathers, nests, and shells.

Their favorite place? It's the pool, they say. "We designed it with the steps running lengthwise, so it's perfect for sunning or lounging with cocktails. It's a great gathering spot for all our friends."

But then they also adore the outdoor living / dining room they created under the romantic length of the pergola and its 17-foot fireplace. "With all the outdoor living spaces, the house seems so much bigger than it actually is."

In short, it's a home for all living styles, all seasons, and all kinds of visitors. The design duo are now looking to bestow their architectural magic on another Shelter Island fixer-upper, but every time they look around this house, they feel too sentimental to leave.

As it all came together, the house became a summary of the things they loved.

The Captain's Mansion

NANTUCKET

Set off the coast of Cape Cod, Nantucket is famous for its maritime history and graceful waterfront architecture. The island is dotted with dozens of grand whaling mansions and stately old homes, many of which were built by wealthy ship captains who once lived here. It is a place that is heavily influenced by the sea – Herman Melville was so inspired by the island that he chose it as the setting for his classic seafaring tale, *Moby-Dick*.

Although it is no longer the major whaling port it was in Melville's day, Nantucket retains the nickname given to it by its early sailors – The Gray Lady of the Sea – because of the fog banks that roll in and the weather-beaten shingles of the island's houses. Both elements combine to create a place that is at once moody and beautiful, quietly elegant and yet inspiring and enlivening at the same time.

Much of Nantucket looks as it did during its whaling days, although the houses are no longer owned by captains and ship merchants, but rather by lawyers, architects and hedge fund millionaires from Boston and New York who fly in for weekends and summer and then fly out again. Indeed, it's rare to find a house that's actually owned by a ship captain anymore – let alone one that's filled with authentic ship memorabilia – but this residence, on the beach at Brandt Point, is just that.

It's a classic Nantucket house, owned by a sea-loving Nantucket family who spend much of their time sailing around the world (and yes, the patriarch was a ship's captain), returning to Nantucket's calm harbor to spend the summers. The house is even situated in the shadow of Brandt Point lighthouse, America's second-oldest lighthouse and a much-loved icon of the island.

The house commands a premium position, right on the sand alongside other grand beachfront homes, but the family didn't want it to stand out or be too visible in an architectural sense. They wanted the house to blend into the landscape and allow the sea view be the star of the show. As such, the front of the property has simply been left as grass rather than becoming landscaped grounds (it's broken only by a path down to the sand), while the rear is only slightly more designed.

When it came to the interior, they wanted something similarly restrained, so they called upon architect William McGuire and his business partner Stephen Theroux of the Nantucket Architecture Group Ltd. to help them create a timeless, quietly refined residence that

was understated in style, yet comfortable and easy to live in. Bill and Stephen, veterans of dozens of Nantucket projects, are famous for their architectural prowess: they are just as adept at caring for old buildings as he is with creating new ones, and he's also aware of the sensitive Nantucket environment. Timeless residences that don't date or decline with age are his signature, and because of it, his firm is in demand all over the island.

This residence is a perfect example of his design sensitivity. The interior may be extensive and the room proportions grand, but it never once feels overwhelming, intimidating or oppressive.

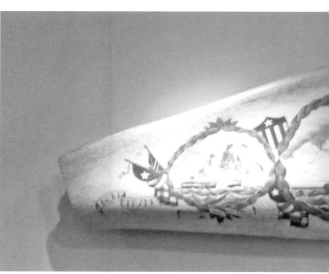

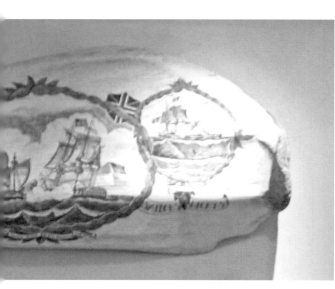

And while it's filled with the owners' collections of art and antiques, it doesn't have a "hands-off" feel when you walk through the displays.

One of the highlights is the entrance to the residence – an elegant gallery-style space featuring built-in display cabinets for the owners' collection of Nantucket baskets, and a handsome, circular rug designed with a compass motif. The impressive stairwell has a soaring ceiling that's curved like the underside of a ship, while the timber stair railings have tiny shells carved into them to continue the maritime theme. The kitchen is an ode to sea blue, with tiles that feature tiny ships on them. Even the family room has a nautical touch, with chaise lounges that have been upholstered in a whimsical ship print.

Much of Nantucket looks as it did during its whaling days, although the houses are no longer owned by captains and ship merchants, but rather by lawyers, architects and hedge fund millionaires from Boston and New York.

The Colonial Home

FLORIDA KEYS

Ah, the Florida Keys ... Was there ever a more extraordinary stretch of coast, a more romantically nostalgic place to be? There are other beaches on America's East Coast, but there is something uniquely fabulous about the Florida Keys. It may be due to the sequence of tiny islands tumbling haphazardly down to Key West. It may be due to the retro feel of the place with its charming 1950s shades of paint, its "Bait, Milk, Tackle" signs, and its low-key, "How's-your-grandad?" kind of manners. It's a laid-back place to be with a touch of 1950s glamour – a world apart from the rest of America, a beautiful, end-of-the-road Brigadoon stuck in a lovely architectural timewarp. And Blue Charlotte is a slice of this enchanting past.

Located on Islamorada (which means "village of islands"), a beautifully unassuming island halfway down the Keys, this rather grand Colonial-style home is part of a larger estate called The Moorings. Famous in many circles, mostly those associated with the architecture, design and hotel crowds, The Moorings is a collection of beach houses owned by architecture lover Herbert Baudoin. Some of them he rents out to visitors. Some of them he keeps for himself.

Blue Charlotte, unfortunately, is one that Herbert Baudoin has chosen (understandably) to keep in the family.

The French businessman bought the oceanfront site in 1988 after washing up on it one day by accident. He took one look at the former coconut plantation, the stretch of white beach, and the island paradise he had stumbled upon, and bought the lot. The property was originally built in 1936 as a private estate and Herbert Baudoin decided to keep it as one, rather than break it into developments, or – horror – a gaudy hotel. So while the beach houses spread across the estate are all individual, both in style and design, together they form a cohesive collection of architectural escapes. The feeling of the estate is of an intimate, wonderfully atmospheric family compound.

Set in lush tropical gardens facing the beach, it's a throwback to a vintage time, and it's no wonder that people such as Ralph Lauren and J. Crew book many of the houses out for their fashion shoots, season after season.

Blue Charlotte is perhaps the most striking of all the houses. Built as a home for his mother, who spends half her year in Africa and the other in France, the gracious, glamorous, Colonial-

inspired home looks like something from Sri Lanka, the Caribbean, or some other British outpost a century ago. It is the largest beach house at The Moorings, and yet it is tucked away at the edge of the property, so its grand lines don't impose on the rest of the place.

The front of the house (which is really the rear, facing the beach) has a façade that's hemmed with two gorgeous wraparound verandas, and accessorized with chic wicker chairs. Inside, a grand living room with a ceiling that rises up two stories feels more homely than you would expect for a space this size. There is also a study, with artifacts from Africa, and various bedrooms for the guests who plead to visit.

The color palette and patterns hark back to Africa, and the soothing chocolates and animal prints add a certain exotic feel to the otherwise laid-back Key West locale.

Outside, a green lawn drifts down to a beach, and then to a photogenic pier dressed with an American flag. (Every other week there is a model being shot here by an enthusiastic photographer and a mesmerized team.)

The real beauty of this place, though, is the understated nature of it. Both Blue Charlotte and The Moorings may be famous, but their feel is still low-key. They're cool, calm, and quietly glamorous – just like the Florida Keys.

Please note that Blue Charlotte is available for professional photo shoots only, however other beach houses in The Moorings are available for rental. Contact www.themooringsvillage.com

It's a laid-back place to be with a touch of 1950s glamour – a world apart from the rest of America, a beautiful, end-of-the-road Brigadoon stuck in a lovely architectural timewarp.

The Elegant Weekender

NANTUCKET

Boston-based interior designer Gary McBournie is becoming an old hand at doing up properties on Nantucket. He has bought and renovated so many on this island over the last 20 years that he has almost become a local.

The designer, who lives in Boston for part of the year, in Florida for part of the year (where he has another office) and on Nantucket for the rest of the time, prefers the quiet beauty of Nantucket's island life. It has, he says, "a heart and soul that you don't find anywhere else." Of course, it's far more remote than his other two homes, but that only adds to its allure and laid-back charm. He also loves the island for its community spirit, its egalitarian friendliness ("everyone mixes with everyone here, regardless of whether you're a millionaire or a builder's apprentice"), and its gentle landscapes, which suit his design aesthetic perfectly.

Gary McBournie's work is known for being quietly sophisticated, but his portfolio is far from uniform. Indeed, his projects over the years have been eclectic and intriguing. The designer is currently working on, among other projects, a boathouse on Nantucket (also in this book), a "camp" in Maine, a loft in Los Angeles, a townhouse in Marlborough and two projects in the West Indies. He's constantly on the go, and

shows no sign of ever slowing down. His reputation is spreading as increasing numbers of people fall in love with his unfussy style. The designer's reputation is so widespread that one day a stranger knocked on the front door of his former home in Nantucket and asked if he would consider selling. The stranger had heard about the designer's design skills from friends and had seen images of the interior of the designer's home, and was happy to pay for the house, lock, stock and furnishings. So the designer, after a moment's pause, said yes, took the not inconsiderable sum offered and bought another property nearby with his partner.

The move must have been something of a shock. The designer went from a fully restored and decorated haven to a gentle wreck of a house. (the designer calls it a "clam shack".) But, designers being designers, he took on the new project with relish.

First, he reconfigured the rooms of the interior so that the floor plan was more sensible and the spaces were more conducive to island life, with clear areas for reading, sitting, drinking and entertaining. The designer transformed the two front rooms, which are linked by two symmetrical doors, into elegant sitting and living rooms decorated in the shades of a

The designer reconfigured
the interior so the spaces
were more conducive
to island life, with clear
areas for reading, sitting,
drinking and entertaining.

Nantucket summer. The walls of both rooms were painted Palladian Blue and the chairs covered in white or turquoise-and-white stripes. The living room was enhanced with touches of tomato red to make it more casual than the sitting area. The bar, which was created by turning a small room into a delightfully inviting space to pour drinks, was dressed in a handsome color scheme of chocolate brown and red that gives it the air of a gentleman's library.

Downstairs, the rooms are linked by elegance and calm. Upstairs, however, is a different matter, and this is where the fun really starts.

For the bedrooms, the designer drew on his love of color. The guest bedroom is now so gorgeous it looks like a miniature room from Versailles. There's even a canopy bed with gold-and-blue stripes that Marie Antoinette would have loved. The principal bedroom is similarly lavish, but in a more restrained way. It has a red and apple-green color palette that makes it come alive while still being comfortable and welcoming.

The red and green color scheme continues outside in the garden where glamorous striped red loungers are placed in the verdant landscape

for most of the summer, inviting guests to lie on them for as long as they please.

There is a sense of calm about this house. It is stylish and obviously well designed, but it is also engaging, inviting and – perhaps most importantly of all for an island hideaway – lively and full of fun. And that, says Gary McBournie, is just what he wanted the house to be.

The Island Idyll

TYBEE ISLAND

What is it about the beach? What is it about the idea of owning a seaside hideaway that prompts so many of us to window-shop for properties on weekends and do drive-bys a flip-flop-throw from the sea? Why is it that the picture of a sandy trail of footsteps up a flight of stairs and a wet beach towel flung over a wooden balustrade will move us more than the sight of a slick city penthouse? And how is it that waves crashing at night, especially accompanied by the satisfying sound of a beer or champagne bottle being opened, will do more for our nerves than any chemical remedy?

There are few things closer to our hearts – or our dreams – than the idea of owning our own great little beach getaway. High-flying businesswoman Diane Willard Kaufman realized this. Several years ago, she stepped back from the pressures of executive life and cross-country travel to purchase a little house on Tybee Island, which is fast acquiring a reputation as an ideal place to stop, sit back and chill out for a while. (Sandra Bullock also owns a house on the island, and the Miley Cyrus film *The Last Song* was recently filmed here.) But sitting back and chilling out wasn't enough for Diane Willard Kaufman – not in the long term anyway. So she came up with a way to combine her love of beach life with business: she launched a company that acts as a portal to all the best beach houses on Tybee Island, and through it, rents beach houses to people who are seeking a slice of island serenity. The mantra for Mermaid Cottages is "Discover the magic in slowing down", and although Diane perhaps isn't the best advocate for this (she still goes a hundred miles an hour in her businesswoman's way!), the beach houses she has in her portfolio certainly encourage a lower speed.

Diane Willard Kaufman's own house on Tybee, Mermaid Manor, is a shining example of how to live the beach life. Okay, there's an office with a phone that seemingly rings non-stop, but the office is in an enclosed porch, which shares space with a fabulous Southern-style sitting area designed for meeting guests, clients or simply serving afternoon tea. Inside, the open living and dining room / kitchen, centered around a fireplace, is decked out with squishy sofas covered in beige-and-white striped fabrics (courtesy of Jane Coslick), vintage cane chairs, antique luggage, and framed botanical and bird prints. With a color palette of sand, white and seaweed, and a definite "beach house" feel (thanks to bare floorboards and stairs, rough-hewn timber panels in the kitchen, and white

timber elsewhere), it immediately encourages residents and visitors to relax – and yes, to chill out. Upstairs, there are more Jane Coslick touches, but the color is brighter – hot pinks and citrus greens feature prominently.

Looking at it, it's hard to believe that this house was once a potential tear-down. In fact, Mermaid Manor was saved when it was moved by Jane Coslick several years ago. It used to sit on the back river with views of the water and sunset, but the new owners of the riverfront property didn't want the inconvenience of a restoration job, and preferred a more modern beach house. So Jane took it away and put it in its present location, where it has blossomed and become a beauty once more.

Diane Willard Kaufman adores it, and so do her two dogs. And it's no wonder. It's a house that makes everyone feel as though they've stepped away from the everyday, even if only for a little while.

For enquiries about Mermaid Manor, look up www.mermaidcottages.com.au

With a color palette of sand, white and seaweed, and a definite "beach house" feel, it immediately encourages residents and visitors to relax.

The Monochrome Home

LONG ISLAND

Interior designer, editor / author, and creative director / principal of her own design company, Tricia Foley is someone who needs no introduction to interior design lovers, particularly those in the blogging world. The author of numerous decorating and lifestyle books and the former editor of many design and lifestyle magazines, she has made her mark on the American design and publishing world for more than 20 years, and is seen as a kind of decorating goddess by many design-loving bloggers. Her reputation has even reached England, where she was recently asked to write the foreword for Christina Strutt's bestselling book *Cabbages and Roses: At Home With Country*.

While much of her reputation has been made in journalism and publishing, notably in editing various design and lifestyle magazines, over the past few years Tricia Foley has also moved into interior design and retail, which was a natural progression of her skills. She has done this at an enchanting Long Island hideaway, a home that has become the perfect place to showcase her spectacular talents.

Although not technically near the beach, Tricia Foley's weekender is considered a coastal getaway, and the Manhattan-based designer treats it as such, retreating to it almost every weekend to wander around the nearby seaside towns or go for long walks along the beach. (It is sufficiently close to Bellport for her to have her toes in the ocean in less than 10 minutes.) The house is also set on a picturesque river, so she has the best of both worlds – bucolic country scenes and breeze-filled beaches.

Tricia Foley is not like most designers. She doesn't go ga-ga for color. Her signature look is a subdued, understated style that she achieves best with black and white – although she also loves natural shades and textures, such as those found in timber, vintage wood, wicker, and old metal pieces. As such, her home is a shrine to black and white and natural style.

Tricia Foley likes to think of it as a modern, fresh take on the country style. Although she's been greatly influenced by the American Colonial and Shaker styles of interior design, she has chosen to create rooms that are bright, light and full of interest. In effect, she's taken a traditional aesthetic and turned it completely on its head, respecting the past while creating an appealing new look for the future. Walls are painted in snow-white shades, floors are left bare, and there's even a fireplace that Tricia Foley has framed in a refined wainscot inspired by a Colonial Williamsburg architectural detail. The

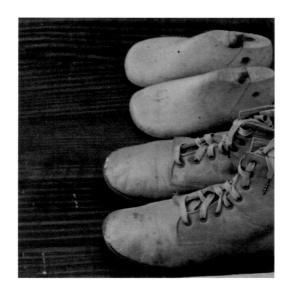

furniture, meanwhile, is simple and functional – think vintage, antique, handmade or rustic; and the colors are muted – whites, wheats, creams, grays, and beiges. Accessories follow a similar theme, and rooms are filled with creamware, silver, natural linens, and Shaker or Scandinavian pieces. There are also glass jars, baskets, vintage luggage, textiles, and calligraphy bits and pieces, all of which are carefully displayed in pared-back collections, as if in a museum.

"I like simplicity," Tricia explains. "I like having just the things I love around me. I find that clutter is distracting and also quite high maintenance. Sometimes, you don't even appreciate what you have, when you have too much around!"

Her understated elegance has attracted a legion of fans some of whom have commissioned the designer to decorate everything from Manhattan lofts to Hamptons beach houses. Some people believe Tricia Foley's next project should be a hotel. It's a fabulous thought, especially if it was somewhere near the calm, serene, white lines of a beach.

Tricia Foley's signature look is a subdued, understated style that she achieves best with black and white – although she also loves natural shades and textures, such as those found in timber, vintage wood, wicker and old metal pieces.

The house is set on a picturesque river, so it has the best of both worlds – bucolic country scenes and breeze-filled beaches.

The Rock Star's Retreat

KEY WEST

What is the modern definition of luxury? Owning your own island would come pretty close. Johnny Depp has one. So too, do Faith Hill, David Copperfield, Sir Richard Branson and Mel Gibson. Even Leonardo DiCaprio has just purchased his own Belize cay. Any star wanting a measure of privacy is now escaping to a far-flung atoll. It's become quite the celebrity rage.

Melody Key was purchased by musician Nick Hexum, front man of the band 311. He wanted a place to retreat to and write music in peace. He found this island, and named it Melody Key. It's a clever play on words because the property is not only a key, but is also located off the coast of Key West. Keys feature everywhere here – no wonder a musician loved it.

The marketing blurb for Melody Key reads: "Ever dream of escaping to a deserted island, where seclusion is paramount and everyday life is left behind?" No, but it's sure got the power of suggestion behind it! (Although you could say the words "private island" to anyone nowadays and most would probably pack up their flip-flops and ask where the keys would be.)

The island is more than five acres in size, and – according to its owner – has a clothing-optional policy. Of course, you don't have to be nude to enjoy the scenery.

The residence was built in 1995 as a unique home consisting of two octagonal structures linked together and surrounded by airy verandas. On the ground floor of the house, there is a large anteroom and a staircase ascending to the living quarters above. The second floor contains the master bedroom and two guest bedrooms, plus French doors leading to an adjoining balcony overlooking the pool, while the third level is for living – and views.

There is also a bar in the top floor's "Great Room", which sits atop a magnificent 300-gallon salt water aquarium stocked with native tropical fish and invertebrates, just in case you don't want to go snorkeling off shore.

And if you need more watery inspiration, there is a final staircase ascending from the kitchen to a crow's nest balcony, where, four stories above the island, there are what Nick Hexum

describes as "unparalleled panoramic views". Considering they're of the Atlantic Ocean, the Gulf of Mexico, and the famous Keys sunrises and sunsets, he may not be far wrong.

Interestingly, Melody's owner has become too busy to escape to his island paradise, and it's now on the market. So if you have a cool US$4.9 million, you, too, could have an island paradise of your very own.

For enquiries about Melody Key (for rental or purchase), contact www.melodykey.com

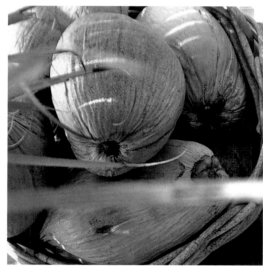

The residence was built in 1995 as a unique home consisting of two octagonal structures linked together and surrounded by airy verandas.

The Writer's Hideaway

TYBEE ISLAND

Writers' houses are often inspirational. They need to be. They are architectural muses for wordsmiths, offering motivation and creative inspiration to searching minds.

This island hideaway, the summer home of bestselling author Mary Kay Andrews, is an example of how a home's design can be enormously influential, in more ways than one. It is so wonderful that it's almost a narrative in itself.

It was restored and remodeled in 2009 by Mary Kay Andrews and her husband, Tom Trocheck, with design consultation from Tybee Island designer Jane Coslick. The name "Breeze Inn" may seem like a throwback to a much-loved cocktail of a certain shade, but it was in fact named as a nod to the fictional Breeze Inn Motel in the writer's *New York Times* bestselling novel, *Savannah Breeze*.

In the novel, the Southern belle BeBe Loudermilk (we're loving the name) loses all her worldly possessions in a brief but disastrous relationship with the gorgeous Reddy, an investment counselor who turns out to be a con man. All that's left in her name is a ramshackle 1950s motor court called Breeze Inn on Tybee Island – an eccentric beach town that calls itself "a drinking village with a fishing problem". In real life, Breeze Inn isn't a motor court but rather a chic beach hideaway, remodeled with a cocktail-style twist

The 1940s-style cottage was fairly spartan, and painted egg-yolk yellow with circus-blue trim, when Mary Kay Andrews and her husband bought it; but it had the potential to be as much of a blockbuster as her books. Their aim was for it to resemble the Florida beach houses of the 1940s. With reclaimed heart pine floors throughout, reclaimed solid-wood doors with antique hardware, painted plank walls, hexagon tiled bathroom floors, and various vintage fixtures, it soon became a stylish and vibrant home. Entered via a cute white picket fence and a garden full of rustling palm trees, scented jasmine and blooming pink roses, the house transports visitors to a bygone era – albeit a very Southern one. Painted in a coolly chic mint shade, its architectural "jacket flap" is a hibiscus-pink front screened door – a fabulous old treasure from a New England antique market.

Inside, the island-bright colors continue with an enclosed apple-green porch, a navy and turquoise living room, and an inspirational

mint-green kitchen. The unifying element is timber, which brings the spaces together in a warm and natural way.

Filled with Jane Coslick's signature shades and Mary Kay Andrews' flea-market finds, it's not so much page-turning as head-turning in a wonderfully colorful way. It's not surprising that another of Mary Kay Andrews' bestsellers was called *The Fixer Upper*. It could have been written in Breeze Inn.

For rental enquiries about Breeze Inn, look up www.mermaidcottages.com

This island hideaway is an example of how a home's design can be enormously influential, in more ways than one. It is so wonderful that it's almost a narrative in itself.

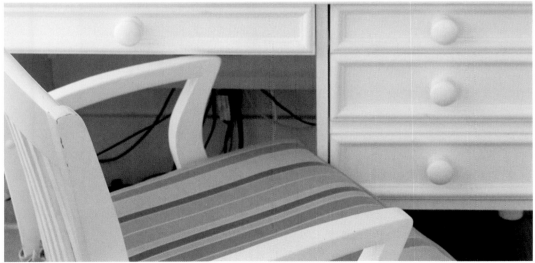

Family Havens

The Designer's Delight

OYSTER BAY, LONG ISLAND

Leading interior designer Jeffrey Bilhuber is well known to many stylish New Yorkers, both within the design industry and outside of it. His is one of those names that crops up in design conversations time and time again. Some people adore his use of color, which is renowned for being glamorously dazzling and often bold. Other people adore his manners and charm, so reminiscent of old-Hollywood stars. Then there are others who adore his homes, which are some of the most envied in the decorating world.

His latest residence is an extraordinary getaway in Oyster Bay on Long Island's North Shore, although calling it a "getaway" is a little like calling Hearst Castle a "hideaway". Named Hay Fever, it's a grand, 17th-century mansion that the designer has transformed into a spectacular weekender for himself, his friends and his much-loved family. Think of *The Great Gatsby* (which was set around here) and then imagine Jay Gatsby's house reworked under the fine touch of a designer with a flair for the dramatic. Now you're getting close to Hay Fever.

If you were to imagine that the house is ostentatious or over-the-top in any way, you'd be wrong. The designer – who grew up in the area and wants his son to share the same

memories of sailing and simple coastal pursuits as he enjoyed when he was a boy – has somehow managed to create a family house that is quietly elegant and yet full of whimsy, color, and life. Sound like a design oxymoron? Not at all. In The designer's hands, a Granny Smith-green sitting room is electric and yet instantly welcoming; a Bloody Mary-red dining room is shocking and yet irresistibly appealing; and a kitchen so enormous that it needs servants and a cook to do it justice feels charming and tailor-made for a modern family.

The stately house, which has also been a private boys' school and a restaurant, was derelict when The designer first spotted it. Surrounded by grand beech trees and lilac, it looked lost to the world. Undaunted, the designer got to work, commissioning his trusted contractor, architect and landscape designer to revive this once-lovely architectural dame and bring her back to life. Set in a "U", with the central courtyard dressed in green lawn and divided by gravel paths, the residence now comprises a main, three-story house and a single-story wing

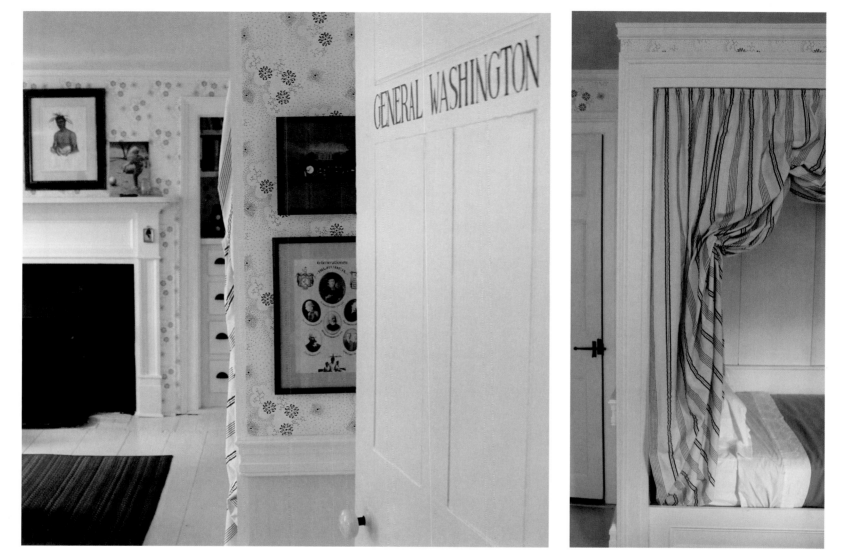

on either side – one housing the luxurious master bedroom and the other the kitchen wing. It's a perfect configuration because the two wings also feature charming covered verandas, and the entire house looks out to a stunning, beautifully designed kitchen garden and an elegant, terraced pool area.

But while the exterior is magnificent, it's the interior where the 'wow' factor really kicks in – and this is all Jeffrey Bilhuber's doing. While the designer consulted with the curators of Monticello and Mount Vernon to determine historically accurate paint colors for some of the interior, the rest is a tribute to his talent and creativity. There is an egg yolk-yellow hall and bathroom that are as inviting as breakfast on a sunny weekend; a hall wallpapered in the color of ripe watermelons; a pale turquoise-and-plum sitting room that somehow works fantastically well; the aforementioned apple-green room; and a main bedroom that is a masterful display of pageantry in red and a glamorous, old-Hollywood beige.

It's a fabulous, flamboyant, wildly imaginative home, and yet it's instantly warm and hospitable too. All you want to do is kick your New York heels off, sink into one of the oh-so-comfortable chairs (pick a room; there are dozens of chic ones to choose from) and hope that Jeffrey comes along with a gin and tonic sometime soon.

Jay Gatsby would have loved it.

It's a fabulous, flamboyant, wildly imaginative home, and yet it's instantly warm and hospitable too.

The Designer's Space

MAINE

Pink is a difficult color to get precisely right. It can be too girlie, too Barbie-doll, or too dull (think dusky-pink-meets-granny's parlor). However, designer Tracey Rapisardi of Sea Rose Designs has discovered a couple of perfect pinks. They're not too princess-y, peach-y, bubble-gum-y, aged or faded. They're clear, exquisitely pretty pinks – like the light of twilight over the beach in summer, or a carefully created cocktail with a mint leaf on the top. Her home is an ode to these perfectly mixed pinks, and there's not a touch of princess in sight!

The designer, who also loves – make that *adores* – turquoise, has used her house to show how wonderful color can be. The lesson begins at the front door, which is edged in sea green, continues via the entrance, which offers a fairy-floss pink sign saying "beach" and a carnival-pink bench to set your shoes upon, and then goes on via a pink, white and turquoise living room to a pale mint-and-white striped bedroom before finishing up in a sitting room that is all shades of the sea. By the end of it you want to go home, buy a can of pale blue tint and redecorate your tired white walls.

The key to this home, which Tracey shares with her husband Richie, who designs and builds most of the furniture for Sea Rose Designs, is that it isn't too sugary sweet, despite the myriad paints. It's gentle, rather than fairground bright, perhaps because it's inspired by the natural colors of the sea rather than fads or whimsy.

It was, says the designer, an attempt to create "an authentic New England beach cottage". To that end, she has succeeded.

"We designed and built the house to be unique, but also enjoyable, fun, cozy, and perhaps a little quaint and quirky too," she explains. "We did this by creating lovely nooks and crannies,

which serve more than one function. We wanted to maximize all the available space, but do it with charm."

As such, the sitting room does double-duty as a living room, the living room does double-duty as a family room, the dining room serves as a breakfast bay, the master bedroom has a study alcove, and the deck is an outdoor living space during the warmer months

"There are so many rooms to escape to, but our favorite room is perhaps the dining room, which has vaulted wood ceilings and white-washed beach beams, plus windows all the way around, and the double French doors that open to the stone terrace, which in turn overlooks the pool. It really feels as though you are outside. You can smell the salty ocean breeze, and hear the sound of the summer waves crash on the white sand."

Attention to detail is everywhere in this house: the beachy glass knobs on the bureaus, the white trims, and the bead board, all of which add additional beach texture. But while it's full of designer detail, the overwhelming feel is that it's an easy place to live in, which is precisely what this duo wanted to achieve.

A beach house is a place
for gathering and having
conversations, and enjoying
each other. It's not a gallery.
It's a place to have fun.

"To me, a beach house equals simple living. It's a place where you can put your sandy toes up and leave wet towels out for the summer sun to dry. One of my favorite things to do is mix fabrics, whether it's a yard found in a store or a remnant from a sewing basket. It makes a place more personal. I also like to have places for collections of shells, rocks and other beach finds for the same reason. A beach house is a place for gathering and having conversations, and enjoying each other. It's not a gallery. It's a place to have fun."

The Gallery Space

SHELTER ISLAND, LONG ISLAND

When you imagine a farmhouse on an island, you imagine a small, fairly humble dwelling, perhaps simple in form, made from rustic materials, with a back-to-basics aesthetic. You don't imagine an elegant gallery where art, design and architecture come together in seamless sophistication. One farmhouse on Long Island, however, has turned rural living on its head – or should that perhaps be on its hammer?

Located on the quiet but spectacularly beautiful Shelter Island, which floats midway between the North Fork and the South Fork, this farmhouse is primarily used as a beach house and weekend getaway by its New York-based family, although in recent years they've come to spend more and more time here. Because they were using it more often, and for large-scale entertaining, they realized that the existing bones of the building were not adequate for their entertaining needs – or for their family's lifestyle. So they called in a design team who were familiar both with beach houses and Shelter Island – SchappacherWhite Ltd.

Steve Schappacher and Rhea White examined the 1908 dwelling, listened to the client's brief (a request for a large-scale living room that opened to an outdoor dining room, a new master bedroom suite, and a garage with an artist's studio above it) and considered the site. They soon realized that any major alterations to the farmhouse in mood, feel, or architectural style would destroy its integrity, and that any new additions might not fit in with the character of the house, or indeed with other existing structures on the property.

The solution? An extension that had its soul in the rustic nature of the farmhouse, but offered a perfect level of luxury living.

"Being from the Midwest, we were inspired by farms that had accumulated different buildings for different purposes over the years, such as the potting shed, the chicken coop, and so on," explains Steve Schappacher. "So we decided to create a living room 'barn' and a bedroom 'shed' that were joined by clear glass passageways. The key was to do it without destroying the façade of the original buildings. So now, even though the house looks quite traditional from the front, the back is not what you would expect at all. Indeed, it's surprisingly open and modern, and yet it stays in character with the original charm of the farmhouse.'

Along with the living room and bedroom buildings, the architects also added a wrap-around porch to the front of the existing house,

It's an intriguing mix of the modern and the traditional, the upscale and the rustic, the farmhouse and the chic Shelter Island hideaway, the spectacular art gallery and the comfortable family home.

which provides a classically beautiful front entrance for visitors as well as a place for people to gather at parties and evening dinners (and they do love gravitating there). And if that wasn't enough "play space", they also designed a spectacular outdoor entertaining area at the rear of the house in the form of a pergola with a soaring ceiling, wonderful long dining table, and exterior fireplace. This entertaining area is reached through a wall of floor-to-ceiling glass in the living room that cleverly opens onto the exterior. This entire area – the indoor living room and the outdoor dining room – creates a memorable gathering place for the many dinner parties the couple love to host.

What's truly fascinating about this house, however, is the materials that have been used – soapstone for the fireplaces, mushroom wood for the walls and ceilings, reclaimed elm for the wide plank flooring (including reproduced "vintage" floor nails), local stacked stone for other walls and fireplaces, and copper for the roof. The decision to use natural materials – woods, stone, and metal – means that they will age gracefully with the house and become more interesting with time.

It's an intriguing mix of the modern and the traditional, the upscale and the rustic, the farmhouse and the chic Shelter Island hideaway, the spectacular art gallery and the comfortable family home. But mostly, it is a wonderful, stylish, inviting place for family and friends to gather away from the city; a place to be inspired, or to simply relax in style.

The Oceanfront Home

MARTHA'S VINEYARD

Looking at this house, it's difficult to guess its age. It could be a hundred years old, or it could be 50. In actual fact, it's slightly over a decade old. That fact comes as a bit of a shock, because it's a house that looks as though it's been comfortably sitting there in the Martha's Vineyard landscape forever.

Built for clients who wanted a no-fuss beach house that was still big enough to house family and friends who came to stay, it is a classic Cape Cod residence – one of those all-American beach houses that everyone loves and envies. There are romantic shingles, a

rambling floor plan and a gambrel roof, all of which give it character and informality; and there are also elegant elements such as columns, which create a slightly dressy and upscale feel. A lovely big porch looks out to the sea, extensive windows capture the ever-changing ocean light from almost every room in the house, and a wonderful stretch of lawn runs down to the beach.

But with the scale and the site came several problems. A grand house can often feel too formal to be truly comfortable in, and the owners were adamant that this house should feel more like an intimate beach house than a spectacular showpiece. They wanted it to be casual and inviting rather than imposing and intimidating, and they wanted something that was easy for a large extended family to live in. They also wanted the sea to be the focus, rather than the architecture or design – the ocean is, after all, right at their front door.

So their brief to their architectural and design team – architect Mark Ferguson, builder Andrew Flake and designer Paula Perlini – was to create a place where the family could feel at home, entertain friends, have easy access to their much-loved things (including all their sports and outdoor gear), and be inspired by the

glorious stretch of beach beyond. A key request, not surprisingly, was for a lovely big veranda, and as many windows as possible without destroying the integrity of the architecture.

The architectural and design team delivered. Answering the call for "family-friendly spaces", Mark Ferguson incorporated not one but two beautiful porch spaces (one downstairs and another upstairs), replaced a formal dining room with an enormous table in the kitchen, designed walls of glorious windows that frame the sea view magnificently, and finished off the house with fabulous rooms that flow from one to the other with such ease that you don't realize you're drifting from the kitchen to the sitting room, or from the sun room to the library.

"We really tried to design a house that was seamless and easy to be in," explains designer Paula Perlini. "For example, some of the more interesting details of the house are the enfilade doors that Mark Ferguson designed, which open from the library through the living room to the kitchen and out to the porch, encouraging a lovely 'flow' of movement. I also used blue right throughout the house, to link the view of the sea with the interior."

There is one exception to this cool color palette – the library. Paula Perlini dressed this dramatic room in a David Hicks-inspired shade of red, which gives the space a sense of theater, then she hung photographs taken in Africa by the owner's wife. The room became an instant gallery of travels as well as an elegant retreat.

There are many small touches that add to the appeal of this house, like sea grass furniture on the porch, which feels fresher and more elegant than wicker, and lots of shell details on the fabrics and accessories, another whimsical nod to the sea.

"It's the kind of house that everyone – family and friends alike – gravitates to, particularly the porch," says Paula Perlini. "Everyone flops out there after sports – tennis, waterskiing, biking, golf. We've tried to create a house that was impressive but not precious. It's a house that encourages long lazy days of sunshine, good food, great memories, and lots of laughter."

The owners were adamant that this house should feel more like an intimate beach house than a spectacular showpiece.

The Stylish Hideaway

MAINE

Many professionally decorated homes look like beautiful magazine photo shoots, but appear completely impractical to live in. Some are minimalist to the point of austerity, while others are decorated to the point of clutter. This house, however, is different. Although decorated by a professional (the talented Tracey Rapisardi), it's been done in such a way that you can easily envisage living here without worrying where the pillows and throws should go. Indeed, you can easily envisage living here without moving a thing.

The residence is located near the coast in Maine, a state that has some of the most dramatic coastline in the country. Surrounded by trees and set on a large block, it has the feel of a private, tucked-away hideaway, but walk in the front door and the mood changes instantly. Inside, it is very much a spacious, modern family home.

The brief for interior designer Tracey Rapisardi was to create "a sanctuary". The house was to be "casual, carefree, and fun, but with a classic upscale look".

Beginning with the architectural bones of the house, the designer set about softening the existing formality of the interior and the enormous proportions of the large-scale rooms by adding architectural details. She then chose a soft, soothing color palette that she used through the whole house.

With the interior leaning firmly toward the upscale and elegant, rather than a casual, comfortable, beach house style, there were challenges in working with the elegance, and enhancing it, rather than playing it down. The floors, for example, are a rich, dark cocoa color – they look magnificent, but have the potential to be too sophisticated for a beach house. So the designer downplayed them slightly by using colorful area rugs throughout. She also painted the floors in some rooms, such as the sunroom, which added a fun, whimsical note.

Another challenge was linking separate parts of the interior, as some rooms were formal while others were clearly designed for weekend use.

The designer solved this by ensuring that all the colors blended from room to room with ease, so that even though the kitchen is predominantly black and white and the sunroom is turquoise striped, they are linked by a pretty, Paris-style pink.

"Parts of this home are bright with fun colors, and other parts are soft and sophisticated, but together they all work well. I've achieved this by carrying over a few of the same colors to the next room."

As a beach house this design works in spectacular fashion, but it's as a family home where it really succeeds.

The brief to the designer was to create an interior that was "casual, carefree, and fun, but still with a classic upscale look".

The Teenager's Place

MAINE

The Cloutier's summer cottage is the kind of escape that feels like a dream. Its design, style, feel, scale, and architectural features are all so perfect, so idyllic, that it's difficult to pinpoint a fault with it. And then suddenly you realize what the negative is: it's not yours.

This bucolic hideaway was inspired by, and predominantly designed for, the Cloutier's children, and their need for a place of their own. The Cloutier family has four of them, you see, and both the kids *and* the adults felt a pressing need for a space to escape the raucous notes of family life, whether for an hour or an entire weekend. They also wanted a place they could take friends or extended family to have parties, swim, cook barbecues, work out, or simply sleep over, particularly during the long lazy days and nights of summer.

It's not surprising that summer features prominently in this family's conversation. Gay Cloutier, who comes from Queensland in Australia's tropical north, desperately misses her childhood home and the pleasures that come from warm-weather living. She makes a point of taking her children back to Australia whenever they can make it, and would love to move back permanently if the option was available. Unfortunately, it's not, so this

irresistible summer house has been built as the next best thing.

The "mini residence" was designed to be a classic New England summer house with understated New England lines. It needed to be both elegant and fun to be in, while still being low maintenance. The starting point for the design was, in fact, the pool – a cool, elegant, watery oasis that offered both inspiration and complications. The idea was to build the cottage level with the pool's surface, so that the pool and its water formed a natural extension of the cottage's living room, and vice versa. This was easier said than done, thanks to the different elevations of the site. The eventual answer was to build the cottage on the same elevation as the pool, but to link it with the higher elevation of the site via a set of interior stairs. These stairs had the additional effect of creating a dramatic entrance: visitors open the front door and step down into the interior, like theatergoers entering a grand auditorium before a play is about to start.

The next step was the interior, and this is where the real magic began. The Cloutier's brief for designer Tracey Rapisardi was "to create a place that was light and airy", so that it would be inviting not only in summer but

The starting point for the design was the pool – a cool, elegant, watery oasis that offered both inspiration and complications.

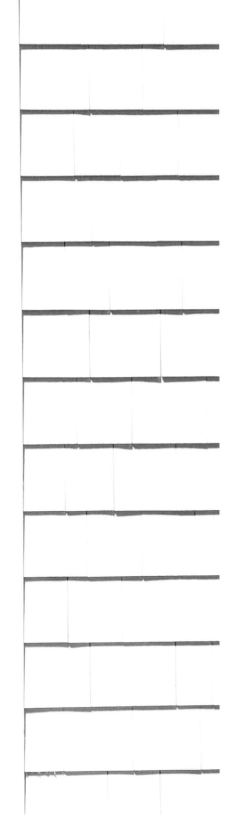

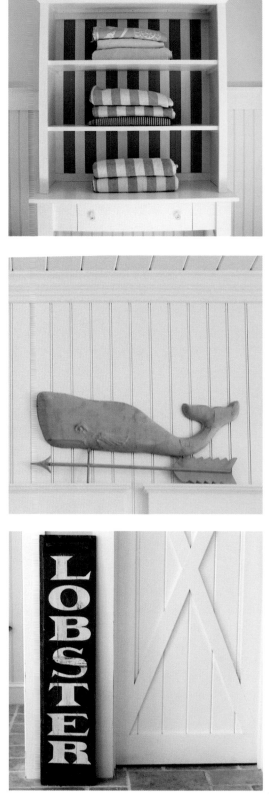

also during the dark days of winter. The Cloutiers also wanted it to be unique, so it would be memorable. And lastly, they wanted a place that was fun to be in, so that it would appeal to teenagers as well as adults.

Taking up the challenge, Tracey Rapisardi began with cool, calm colors inspired by the sea, such as turquoise greens and sea-glass blues. She then gave the interior a slightly whimsical touch by selecting fun and quirky furnishings, features, and fabrics that make people smile.

The designer's flair for decorating is famous – her projects are often featured in magazines for their unexpected wit, whimsy, and their bold, look-at-me color palettes. But she is also talented at paring elements back so that spaces remain uncluttered and easy on the eye. This project showcases her skill for pairing the understated with the theatrical.

The simple kitchen, for example, is a quiet space enhanced by white wainscoting and "dressed" in whimsical extras such as star cutouts and shutter-style cabinet doors. The cute dressing room also features wainscoting outfitted with delightful hooks – a handy spot for colorful pool towels. And the breakfast nook, which has crisp white shutters and a banquette trimmed in white wainscoting, has similarly intriguing touches such as pastel stripes painted on the table.

Unique Beach Retreats

The Artist's Getaway

LONG ISLAND

How to describe Rick Livingston's and Jim Brawders' beach house? For a start, it is surely one of the most unusual beach houses in America. Set right on the beach at Quogue, halfway down Long Island, on a gentle curve of a sand dune, it's reached by a rambling road that wanders off the main road and then down an enchanting sandy track through the trees. At the end of this track, sitting low in the landscape, is the house. Or rather, the barn – sort of. It's difficult to describe exactly what it is.

It has the traditional lines, shape, and ceiling height of a classic barn, but its position, its windows, and its exterior porch suggest it might be something more. It's a house with a sense of mystery.

The structure was built a century ago in Maryland as a Navy recreation hall. It was cut into pieces, moved by rail and truck, and reassembled on the beach by a family who owned much of the land in the region. The building was used as a casual getaway for many years, and was particularly loved by the artists and creatives in the family for its coastal inspiration and its box-seat proximity to the beach.

Fast-forward many years to the day Manhattan-based designer Rick Livingston, and his partner

Jim stumbled across it. The house was available as a rental by this time, and they decided to rent it with some friends for the summer. They loved it so much they returned the following summer, and the following summer, eventually racking up more than two decades of vacations in the character-filled old home. Although the property had been owned by the same family since the nearby village was founded in 1659, the owners eventually decided to sell. When they did, Rick and Jim took one look at each other, counted their money, and bought the lot.

Then, rather than tearing the place down to make way for a more modern, edgy, architectural abode, they decided to retain the old barn feel and simply upgrade it to make it into a more comfortable escape. The unusually high roofline, so reminiscent of a barn, was retained and enhanced with beautifully whimsical pieces, such as a collection of bright orange bird cages (bought for a summer party and never taken down) and a fabulous rope chandelier. The enormous room that drifts on through the building was separated into sections with a central fireplace and distinct seating areas, offering reading nooks beside windows, a study corner, a cozy lounge, and a lovely dining room beside the kitchen. The bedrooms,

meanwhile, were left dressed in their timber finishes but decorated by Rick Livingston in a soothing color palette that matched the soft grassy greens, pale blues, and driftwood shades of the beach outside. He is a master at orchestrating colors, textures, forms, and materials, and this was a place where he could go to town. Wonderfully quirky touches are everywhere you look – old postcards sent to Rick Livingston's family over the years are plastered over the old wardrobe in the master bedroom; vintage glass bottles filled with collected shells make up a "display shelf" in the bathroom; miniature ships – a passion of Jim's – are artfully arranged on the living room walls; and vintage buoys create interest near the study.

But transforming this old building into a stylish new home was not just about creating elegant interiors with a rustic touch; the new owners also wanted to focus on the building's relationship to the outside world and its physical and emotional connection to the surrounding landscape. Exterior areas such as a front porch, a rear veranda, a sun deck, an outdoor shower, and a dune deck are integral to the house because they create a natural flow between inside and out, between man-made and landscape forms. It's a house that allows its owners to wander outside and embrace nature, but also withdraw into the building, light the fire and bunker down while the rain and sea spray pounds down outside.

They now escape here whenever they can during the summer and love nothing more than sharing it with friends and family season after season. It is a timeless hideaway, traditional yet modern, cozy yet impressive, and spectacular yet still warm and welcoming. In a word, it is glorious.

It's a house that allows its owners to wander outside and embrace nature, but also withdraw into the building, light the fire and bunker down while the rain and sea spray pounds down outside.

The Grand Waterfront Home

NANTUCKET

When a house is featured in *Architecture Digest*, you know it's special. This house, however, is *particularly* special. Adjoining 300 acres of conservation land on one of Nantucket island's highest points overlooking Nantucket Sound, it is a spectacular example of what can happen when a talented architect meets a truly astounding site.

The 28-room house is the dream of two successful Hollywood power brokers, Stephen and Mary Meadow, who fell in love with Nantucket one year and decided to relocate much of their life from Beverly Hills to the East

Coast island. They already had a house on the island but had outgrown it, thanks to a rapidly expanding extended family, so they bought six acres near the sea for a larger residence that would accommodate all their needs.

Enter William McGuire of Nantucket Architecture Group Ltd. After visiting the site, which is far from the built-up village scene of Nantucket town and has stunning sweeping views, Bill McGuire decided to create a residence that complimented the landscape rather than interfered with it. He built a house that sits slightly down in a natural hollow, but

Enormous windows frame the beautiful vistas, while out in the garden, strategically placed entertaining areas and paths allow for lines of sight straight up to the house.

still takes advantage of the magical rural and sea views. It may seem impossible – the three-story residence is rather grand, after all – but the design of the house is such that it doesn't impose on the natural landscape.

Everything about the design of this property is geared towards the views, whether it's the views of the surrounding area or views of the house itself. Inside, enormous windows frame the beautiful vistas, while out in the garden, strategically placed entertaining areas and paths, including a coolly glamorous pool, allow for lines of sight straight up to the house.

The residence consists of three stories. On the lower level there is a wine cellar, a massage room, a movie theater, a gym, a steam room, and a game room with a pool table. From here, a spectacular floating spiral staircase ascends to the main level, where there is a grand living room ("the great room") that has antique beams, a wide-plank oak floor and a large stone fireplace (one of six in the house). On this level there is also is an enormous kitchen, an equally enormous family room, plus an enchanting indoor / outdoor covered veranda, which is the most used room in the house in summer. The staircase then winds its way up to the next floor, where the master suite is located. A separate staircase leads to bedrooms for their children and grandchildren.

The interior is flecked with folk art that has been collected by both the owners and interior designer Karin Blake, and includes whimsical pieces such as a carousel lion, a carved antique sign for a tavern called the Raven & Ring, a copper cow weathervane, and a six-foot-tall 19th-century English pond boat that hangs above the mantel in the den.

The Historic Home

MARTHA'S VINEYARD

For a beach house to succeed, it has to be used, it has to be loved, and it has to be lived in – and regularly, not just once or twice every summer. It has to be a place where people can kick off their flip flops or sandshoes, tread across the floorboards, make themselves a sandwich and continue out to a porch or deck, leaving a trail of flotsam and jetsam in their wake. It has to be a house that embraces this casual living, and doesn't shy away from use.

This gracious waterfront home, built in 1890, is a classic beach house in every sense. It's not only beautifully aged and beautifully designed, but also beautifully positioned, right on the sea at Edgartown. However, like a grand old society dame who doesn't really want to reveal her age or her secrets of youth, it's also had "a little work done". Midway through the 1990s, the owners realized that the property required significant renovations, so in 1995 they decided to rebuild. Concerned that any renovations would destroy the character and gracious nature of the house, and perhaps even its architectural integrity, the owners hired architects Mark Hutker and Michael van Valkenburgh, builder Andrew Flake, and interior designer Paula Perlini. Their brief was to upgrade the home, but to do it in such a way that the changes would feel as though "they had always been there".

The design team happily complied. The result is a stunning and contemporary beach house hidden inside a gracious, turn-of-the-century island residence.

One of the more interesting aspects of the house is its circular theme, which follows the contour of the land. Even the hedge-lined driveway is designed in a circular shape. There is also a three-step, bleacher-like front porch that continues the curving, layered theme, and gives the family a place from which to watch the ever-changing show of the ocean.

The owners, however, love the interior the most, and it's easy to see why. Redressed in crisp white woodwork and enhanced with splendid window seats looking out to sea, it's a space that's simply irresistible. Indeed, it's so irresistible that not only do friends and family love to come and stay, but the owners themselves find it difficult to leave at the end of summer and vacation breaks.

It is now a house for entertaining and gathering, but it is also a house for reading and dreaming. More importantly, it is a house that encompasses everyone – adults, children, neighbors, friends and even dogs – with absolute ease.

It is now a house for entertaining and gathering, but it is also a house for reading and dreaming.

The Movie House

TYBEE ISLAND

It's not often that a house inspires a movie. Usually the movie is scripted first, then a house – whether real or a constructed set – is found to film the movie in. But in the case of *The Last Song*, the 2010 film starring Miley Cyrus and Greg Kinnear, a remarkable beach house proved to be so memorable that the directors decided to turn it into one of the stars of the story.

Set right on the beach on tiny Tybee Island off the coast of Savannah in the state of Georgia, the two-story, six-bedroom, classic rambling beach residence has been in one family for almost a century. It was built in 1911 and much of the house is still as it was when it was first constructed, including the floor plan, the original timber paneling, the bathrooms and bedrooms, the kitchen and servery, and the delightfully wide, wrap-around porches that allow ocean breezes to sweep through the enormous rooms.

Its beautifully preserved character and architectural integrity are unusual for a house of this age on this island, and are so charming that when *The Long Song's* location scouts saw it after three months of fruitless searching for the perfect residence, they immediately knew that this place was their dream set.

"It's almost a character in itself," said scout Andy Young of the choice to move much of the film here. The beachfront location with its extraordinary views had enormous potential for shooting scenes, while the surrounding island, with its home-spun charm and quaint clapboard cottages, offered yet more glorious backdrop beauty for the director to work with.

The house's owner, Sam Adams, agreed with the location scouts – it was indeed a perfect house for filming – but he had another reason for allowing the film crew in. He wanted to immortalize his family's beloved old beach house in case it was destroyed by storms. He wanted the house to be remembered in case there came a day when its age and its vulnerable location, right on the beach at the end of the island, contributed to its eventual demise.

Ironically, the film crew felt that the house wasn't battered enough for filming, and set about making it even more weathered and old. In order to fit in with the storyline, it had to look like a house that had been uncared for over the years, so the film crew transformed both the façade and the interior of the house to reflect its fictional owner's neglect.

The outside of the house had been updated with stark white trim, black shutters, and vinyl screens, and the team softened and aged these elements to make the house look more like an "authentic" old beach house. They also reconfigured some of the rooms, partly to allow for ease of filming but also to make the floor plan simpler and less rambling.

Of course, the house was turned back into its old self after filming finished, and returned lock, stock, and timber panel intact to its owners. All of the set furniture was removed and the family's original furniture, including the lovely old timber chairs, antique dining table, iron beds, and chaise lounges were returned to their original spots, where they had happily sat for years. Now, it is once again a family beach house: casual, relaxed, slightly rustic, utterly comfortable, and full of wonderful memories.

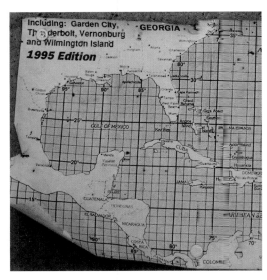

Its beautifully preserved character and architectural integrity are unusual for a house of this age.

Acknowledgments

The Images Publishing Group and Janelle McCulloch would like to acknowledge and sincerely thank the following architecture firms, design companies and individuals for their gracious assistance in the production of this book.

Sam Adams and the Adams family; Hubert Baudoin, Thomas Gibson and Robyn Ross of The Moorings; Jeffrey Bilhuber and Rachel Klein of Bilhuber & Associates; the Cloutier family; Joe and Jane Coslick and Anna Speir of Jane Coslick Designs and Restorations; Darcy Creech of Peter Beaton Studio; Tricia Foley of Tricia Foley Design; Jim Heflin of Tybee Cottages; Nick Hexum; the Hommert family; the Horvitz family; the Israel family; Rick Livingston and Jim Brawders of Period Interior Design; Erica and Ava Mayo; Gary McBournie and Bill Richards of Gary McBournie Inc.; William (Bill) McGuire and Stephen Theroux of the Nantucket Architecture Group Ltd; the Meadow family; Scott Miller and Jill Eatz; Paula Perlini of Paula Perlini Inc.; Tracey and Richie Rapisardi of Sea Rose Designs; Edward and Christine Sanford; Steve Schappacher and Rhea White of Schappacher White; Diane Willard Kaufman and Mary Kay Andrews.

For queries regarding the properties featured in this book please refer to the following websites:

The Chic Beach Shack – Splash Shack
www.tybeecottages.com

The Chic Weekender – Bead Cottage
www.tybeecottages.com

The Colonial Home – Blue Charlotte at The Moorings
(please note Blue Charlotte is available for photo shoots only, however other beach houses in The Moorings are available for rental) www.themooringsvillage.com

The Designer's Space – Rapisardi House
(for sale) www.searosedesigns.com

The Island Idyll – Mermaid Manor
www.aerodrome.com/Mermaid_Boathouse or email jill@aerodrome.com

The Photogenic Boathouse – Lydia Boathouse
www.nantucketonline.com or www.greatpointproperties.com

The Rock Star's Retreat – Melody Key
(for sale) www.melodykey.com

The Seaside Hideaway – 99 Steps
www.tybeecottages.com

The Writer's Hideaway – Breeze Inn
www.mermaidcottages.com

To contact the architects and designers featured in this book please refer to:

Bilhuber & Associates
www.bilhuber.com Ph: +212 308 4888

Gary McBournie Inc.
www.gmcbinc.com Ph: +617 542 5700

Jane Coslick Designs and Restorations
www.janecoslick.com Ph: +912 354 8602

The Nantucket Architecture Group Ltd
www.nantucketarchitecture.com Ph: +508 228 5631

Paula Perlini Inc.
www.paulaperlini.com Ph: +212 889 6551

Period Interior Design (Period NYC)
www.period-nyc.com Ph: +212 352 9400

Peter Beaton Studio
www.peterbeaton.com Ph: +508 228 8456

Schappacher White
www.schappacherwhite.com Ph: +212 279 1675

Sea Rose Designs
www.searosedesigns.com Ph: +207 799 3508

Tricia Foley Design
www.triciafoley.com

Index

The information and illustrations in this publication have been prepared and supplied by Janelle McCulloch. While all reasonable efforts have been made to ensure accuracy, the publishers do not, under any circumstances, accept responsibility for errors, omissions and representations express or implied.